J
910
Our

World Book's Learning Ladders

Our Planet's Pieces

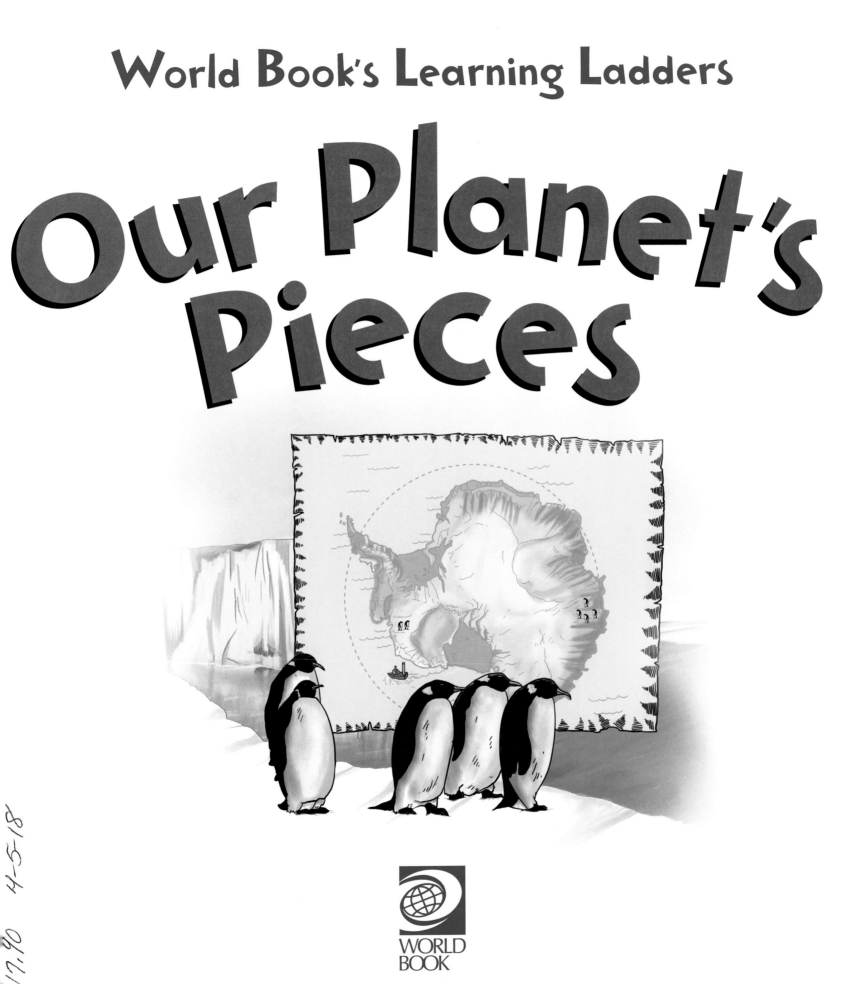

WORLD
BOOK

www.worldbook.com

World Book, Inc.
180 North LaSalle Street
Suite 900
Chicago, Illinois 60601
USA

For information about other World Book publications, visit our website at **www.worldbook.com** or call **1-800-WORLDBK (967-5325).**

For information about sales to schools and libraries, call **1-800-975-3250 (United States); 1-800-837-5365 (Canada).**

Library of Congress Cataloging-in-Publication Data for this volume has been applied for.

World Book's Learning Ladders
ISBN 978-0-7166-7945-5 (set, hc.)

Our Planet's Pieces
ISBN 978-0-7166-7951-6 (hc.)

Also available as:
ISBN 978-0-7166-7961-5 (e-book)

Printed in China by Shenzhen Wing King Tong Paper Products Co, Ltd., Shenzhen, Guangdong
1st printing December 2017

Staff

Executive Committee
President: Jim O'Rourke
Vice President and Editor in Chief: Paul A. Kobasa
Vice President, Finance: Donald D. Keller
Vice President, Marketing: Jean Lin
Vice President, International Sales: Maksim Rutenberg
Vice President, Technology: Jason Dole
Director, Human Resources: Bev Ecker

Editorial
Director, New Print Publishing: Tom Evans
Senior Editor, New Print Publishing: Shawn Brennan
Writer: S. Thomas Richardson
Director, Digital Product Content Development: Emily Kline
Manager, Indexing Services: David Pofelski
Manager, Contracts & Compliance (Rights & Permissions):
   Loranne K. Shields
Librarian: S. Thomas Richardson

Digital
Director, Digital Product Development: Erika Meller
Digital Product Manager: Jonathan Wills

Graphics and Design
Senior Art Director: Tom Evans
Coordinator, Design Development and Production: Brenda Tropinski
Senior Visual Communications Designer: Melanie J. Bender
Senior Cartographer: John M. Rejba
Media Researcher: Rosalia Bledsoe

Manufacturing/Pre-Press
Manufacturing Manager: Anne Fritzinger
Proofreader: Nathalie Strassheim

Photographic credits: Cover: © FatCamera/iStockphoto; © Dreamstime: 11; Oregon State University (licensed under CC BY-SA 2.0): 11; © Shutterstock: 4, 7, 8, 9, 12, 13, 14, 15, 16, 17, 18, 19, 20, 21, 23.

Illustrators: WORLD BOOK illustrations by Quadrum Ltd

What's inside?

This book tells you about the seven continents of our Earth. You'll learn about different buildings, land, weather, animals, and cities around the world!

Our continents

Earth is round, like a giant ball. It has seven big pieces of land called continents *(KON tuh nuhnts)*. They are Africa, Antarctica, Asia, Australia, Europe, North America, and South America. Around the continents are five huge areas of water. These are called the Arctic Ocean, Atlantic Ocean, Indian Ocean, Pacific Ocean, and Southern Ocean. World maps are flattened pictures of the planet's outside. The lines help people find places on the map.

Arctic Ocean

NORTH AMERICA

Atlantic Ocean

Equator

Pacific Ocean

SOUTH AMERICA

A **globe** is a hollow (empty) round ball with a world map on it. Only a round globe can show a true picture of the surface (outside) of our round Earth.

The **South Pole** is at the bottom of the world.

The **North Pole** is at the top of the world.

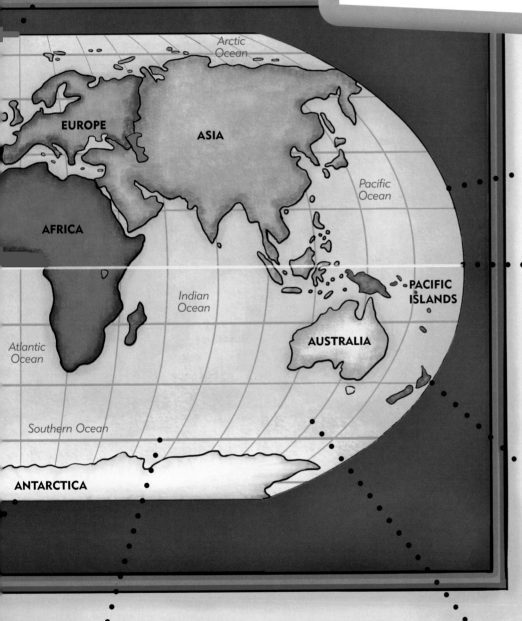

The area north of the equator is called the **Northern Hemisphere.**

The **equator** is a line of latitude that goes around the middle of Earth. It is halfway between the North Pole and the South Pole.

The region south of the equator is called the **Southern Hemisphere.**

Lines on a map that run east-west are called **lines of latitude** *(LAT uh tood).*

Lines on a **map** that run north-south are called **lines of longitude** *(LON juh tood).*

Moving around

Scientists say Earth's crust, or outside, is made of huge pieces called plates. The plates sit on melted rock. The melted rock moves slowly, making the plates move, too. When the plates move, they can push against each other to make mountains and valleys.

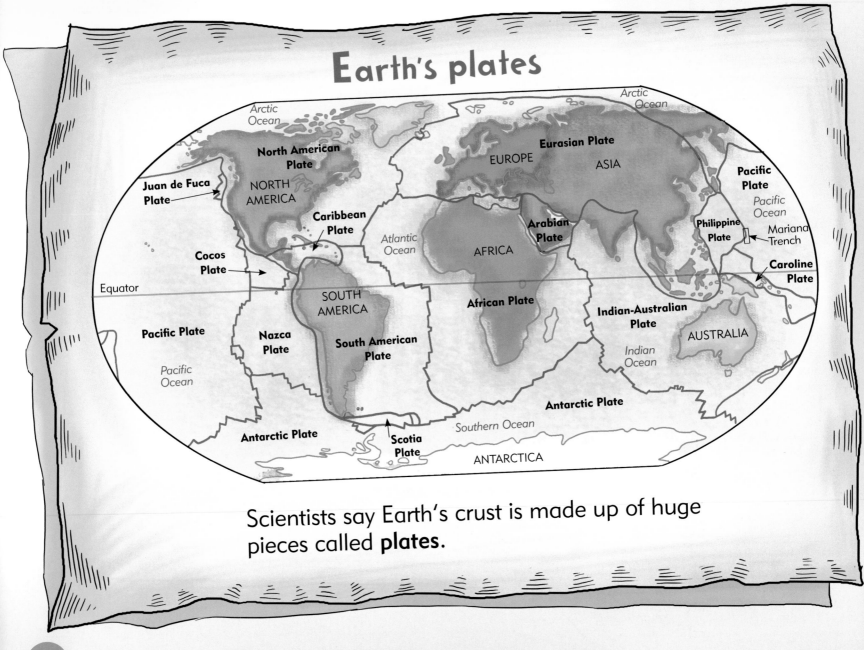

Earth's plates

Scientists say Earth's crust is made up of huge pieces called **plates**.

Mountains

The Himalaya (*HIH muh LAY uh*), is Earth's highest **mountain** system. It was formed by two plates pushing against each other.

Volcanoes

Moving plates can make **volcanoes** erupt. This can also cause earthquakes.

Trenches

The Mariana Trench is the deepest place on Earth. The **trench** was made when plates moved. A trench is a huge valley.

Africa

Africa goes from the Mediterranean Sea in the north to the Cape of Good Hope in the south. It touches the Atlantic Ocean in the west and the Indian Ocean in the east. Scientists think the earliest humans lived in Africa about 2 million years ago.

The Sahara *(suh HAR uh)* is the world's largest **desert**.

The imaginary line called the **equator** goes though the middle of Africa.

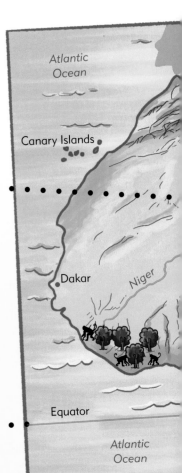

Because it is so big, Africa has many kinds of land. **Grasslands** are the home of many animals, such as zebras (shown), elephants, giraffes, and buffaloes.

Mountain **monkeys** like this live in Africa's rain forests.

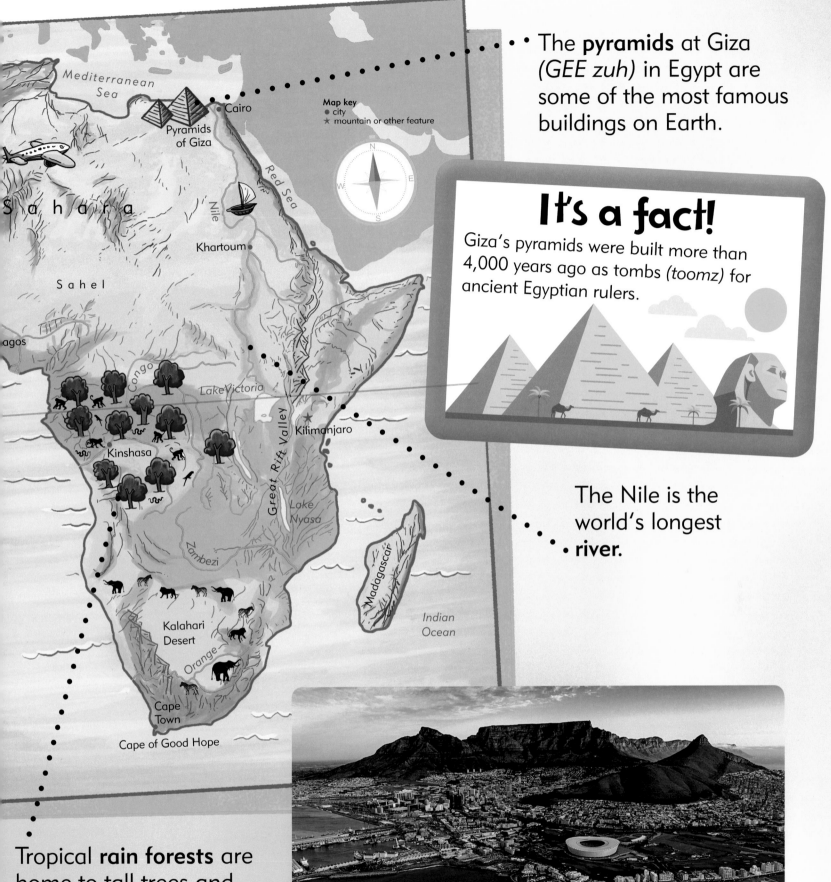

The **pyramids** at Giza *(GEE zuh)* in Egypt are some of the most famous buildings on Earth.

Mediterranean Sea

Cairo

Pyramids of Giza

Map key
● city
★ mountain or other feature

Sahara

Nile

Red Sea

Khartoum

Sahel

agos

Congo

Lake Victoria

Great Rift Valley

Kilimanjaro

Kinshasa

Lake Nyasa

Madagascar

Zambezi

Indian Ocean

Kalahari Desert

Orange

Cape Town

Cape of Good Hope

It's a fact!

Giza's pyramids were built more than 4,000 years ago as tombs *(toomz)* for ancient Egyptian rulers.

The Nile is the world's longest **river.**

Tropical **rain forests** are home to tall trees and many kinds of plants and animals.

Table Mountain is a landmark in the nation of South Africa. It is a flat-topped mountain that rises above the city of Cape Town.

Antarctica

Antarctica *(ant AHRK tih kuh)* is the coldest place on Earth. Thick layers of ice cover most of the land. Freezing, icy waters are all around the continent. Huge glaciers *(GLAY shuhrz)*—thick sheets of ice that move slowly—cover Antarctica's mountains.

South Atlantic Ocean

Antarctic Circle

Southern Ocean

Indian Ocean

Weddell Sea

Queen Maud Land

Ronne Ice Shelf

SOUTH POLE

Transantarctic Mountains

Marie Byrd Land

Ross Ice Shelf

Wilkes Land

South Pacific Ocean

Ross Sea

Map key
★ mountain or other feature

Antarctica covers the **South Pole.**

These emperor **penguins** cannot fly, but they are fast swimmers!

An **ice shelf** is a thick, floating piece of ice that is made when glaciers reach the ocean.

The Atlantic, Indian, Pacific, and Southern **oceans** are between Antarctica and the rest of the world.

Ships coming to Antarctica must steer around tall icebergs and break through huge **ice fields** to reach land.

Scientists have places on Antarctica called research stations. The scientists study the continent's plants, ice, and rocks.

It's a fact!

At the South Pole, the sun stays in the sky for 90 days before and 90 days after December 21. The sun cannot be seen for 90 days before and 90 days after June 21.

Asia

Asia is Earth's largest continent. Asia goes all the way from Africa and Europe in the west to the Pacific Ocean in the east. The northernmost part of the continent is in the frozen Arctic. In the south, Asia ends near the equator, where it is very hot. Asia has more land and more people than any other continent.

The Arabian Peninsula is a large desert area. A **peninsula** is a piece of land that has water almost all the way around it.

It's a fact!

About 5,500 years ago, people living in a part of Asia called Mesopotamia (*MEHS uh puh TAY mee uh*) built the world's first cities.

Map key
● city
★ mountain or other feature

Ural Mountains

Caucasus Mts.

Caspian Sea

Mesopotamia

Tian Shan

Hindu Kush

Plateau of Tibet

Himalaya

Arabian Peninsula

Dubai

Karachi

Delhi

Mt. Everest

Arabian Sea

Kolkata

Mumbai

Deccan

Bay of Bengal

Indian Ocean

Some of the largest, busiest, and most modern **cities** in the world are in Asia. Millions of people live and work in Dubai in the United Arab Emirates.

Mount Everest is the highest **mountain** in the world. It stands 29,035 feet (8,850 meters) tall.

★ NORTH POLE

Arctic Ocean

S i b e r i a

Sea of Okhotsk

G o b i

Manchurian Plain

Great Wall of China

Beijing

Tokyo

Seoul

Pacific Ocean

Shanghai

East China Sea

Hong Kong

Pacific Ocean

Manila

South China Sea

Bangkok

Equator

Singapore

Borneo

Sumatra

Jakarta

The Ural Mountains go for thousands of miles or kilometers through western Russia. Many geographers think the mountains are a natural boundary (border) between Europe and Asia.

The Great Wall of China was built across thousands of miles or kilometers in north-central China.

Thousands of **islands** are part of Asia.

Australia

Australia is the only continent that is also a country. It is the smallest continent. It is famous for its unusual animals, such as the kangaroo, the koala, and the wallaby. Australia is south of the equator. For that reason, it is sometimes called the land "down under."

Australia's rough land is sometimes called the **outback.** Few people live in the outback. But many unusual animals, like these **kangaroos,** do!

Darwin

Arnh Lan

Indian Ocean

Great Sandy Desert

Tanami Desert

Alice Spri

Gibson Desert

Uluru

Great Victoria Desert

Darling Range

Perth

Nullarbor Plain

Great Australian Bight

Uluru (*OO loo roo*) is a large rock in central Australia. It is important to Australia's native people. It is also known as Ayers Rock.

The Great Barrier Reef is the world's largest group of **coral reefs**. This underwater place is in the Pacific Ocean off Australia's northeastern coast. The reef is home to thousands of animals, like these colorful clownfish

The Sydney Opera House is one of Australia's most famous landmarks.

It's a fact!

Australia's Aboriginal (AB uh RIHJ uh nuhl) peoples were its first settlers. Aboriginal people may have lived in Australia for as long as 50,000 years.

The Great Victoria Desert is Australia's largest **desert**.

The **island** of Tasmania is part of Australia.

Europe

Europe is one of the smallest continents. It goes from the Arctic Ocean in the north to the Mediterranean Sea in the south. It has deep valleys, land that is good for farming, and rocky coastlines. There are many forests, rivers, and mountains, like the Alps in Europe.

Thousands of **islands** in the Atlantic Ocean and Mediterranean Sea are part of Europe.

Europe has ancient ruins, old **castles**, historic towns, and modern cities. You can visit this castle named Neuschwanstein *(noy SHVAHN shtyn)* Castle in Bavaria, Germany. A king once lived here.

There are many open areas in Europe called grazing lands where animals roam. These **sheep** in Scotland graze (feed) on grasses.

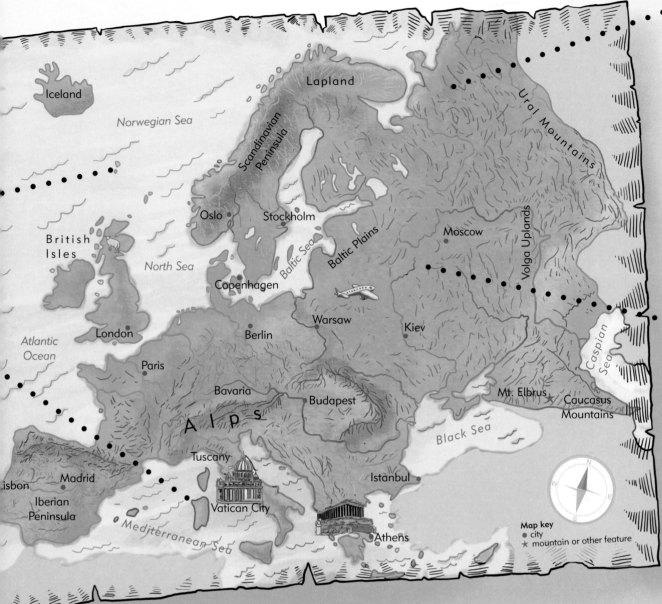

Russia is the largest **country** on Earth. It is partly in Europe and partly in Asia.

Asia and Europe are part of the same huge **piece of land**.

Map key
- city
★ mountain or other feature

Ancient Greece was one of the world's great civilizations (communities). The Greeks did important things in art, science, and government.

It's a fact!

Vatican City is the smallest country in the world. It is completely inside the city of Rome, Italy.

17

North America

North America includes Canada, Greenland, the United States, Mexico, Central America, and the islands of the Caribbean Sea. It is bordered by the Pacific Ocean in the west and the Atlantic Ocean in the east. The continent has icy areas in the north and sunny beaches in the south. There are many forests, deserts, and jungles.

It's a fact!

The earliest North Americans were American Indians. They came to the continent from Asia thousands of years ago. At that time, a small strip of land connected Asia and Alaska.

The Grand Canyon, in the southwestern United States, is one of the most amazing places in the world. The **canyon** was slowly formed by a river cutting down through the rock over millions of years.

Many kinds of animals live in different areas of North America. Animals like moose (shown), beavers, and ducks live in forests. Caribou, polar bears, and seals live in cold areas. Warm areas are home to jaguars, monkeys, and rattlesnakes.

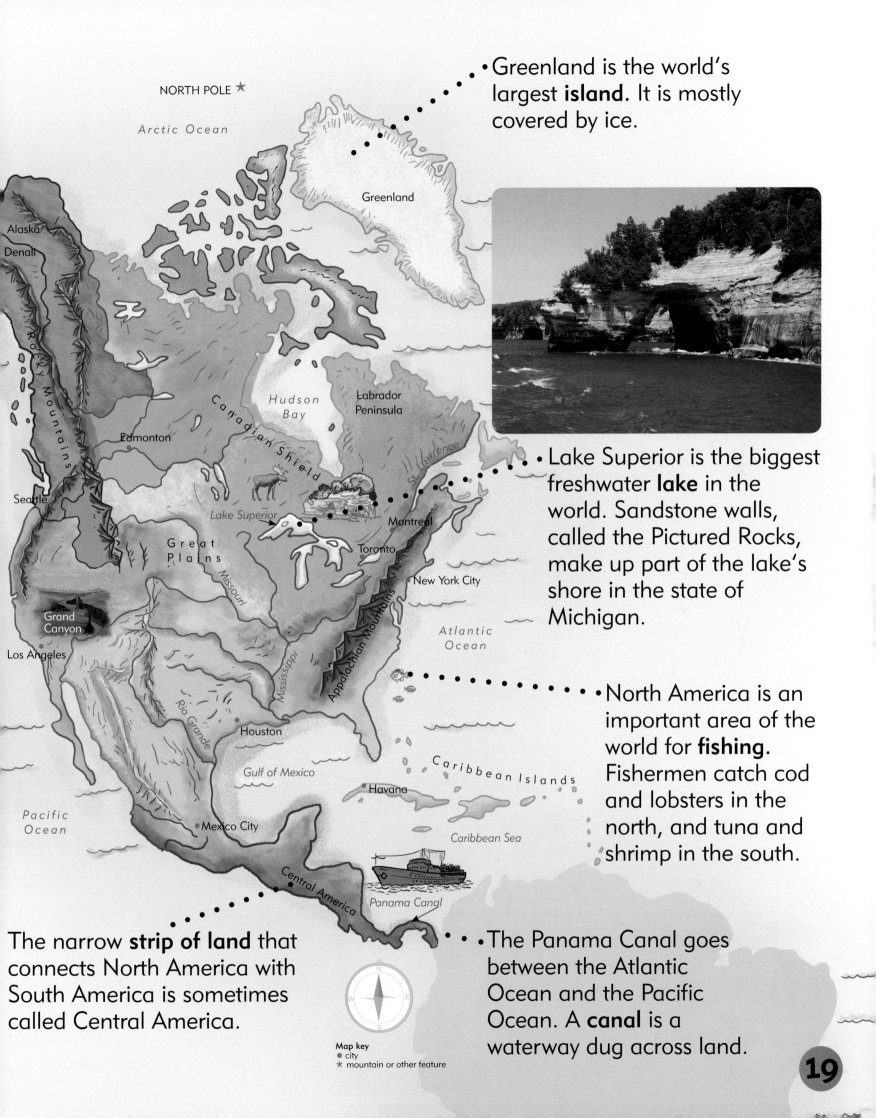

NORTH POLE ★

Arctic Ocean

Greenland is the world's largest island. It is mostly covered by ice.

Greenland

Alaska

Denali

Rocky Mountains

Canadian Shield

Hudson Bay

Labrador Peninsula

Edmonton

Seattle

Lake Superior

Lake Superior is the biggest freshwater lake in the world. Sandstone walls, called the Pictured Rocks, make up part of the lake's shore in the state of Michigan.

St. Lawrence

Montreal

Toronto

Great Plains

New York City

Missouri

Grand Canyon

Los Angeles

Appalachian Mountains

Atlantic Ocean

North America is an important area of the world for fishing. Fishermen catch cod and lobsters in the north, and tuna and shrimp in the south.

Mississippi

Rio Grande

Houston

Gulf of Mexico

Havana

Caribbean Islands

Mexico City

Caribbean Sea

Pacific Ocean

Central America

Panama Canal

The narrow strip of land that connects North America with South America is sometimes called Central America.

The Panama Canal goes between the Atlantic Ocean and the Pacific Ocean. A canal is a waterway dug across land.

Map key
● city
★ mountain or other feature

19

South America

South America has nearly every kind of land and weather. It goes from Central America in the north to the tip of Cape Horn in the south. South America is bordered by the Pacific Ocean on the west and the Atlantic Ocean on the east. It has tall mountains, dark jungles, and rolling plains.

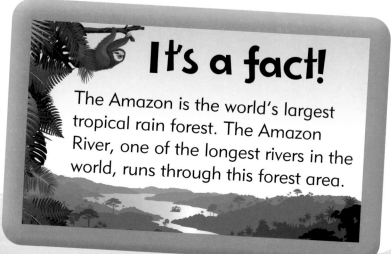

It's a fact!

The Amazon is the world's largest tropical rain forest. The Amazon River, one of the longest rivers in the world, runs through this forest area.

The Andes Mountains go for thousands of miles or kilometers through western South America. Many of these **mountains** are volcanoes. • • • •

Machu Picchu (MAH choo PEEK choo) is a stone **ruin** in the mountains of Peru. It was probably a home for rulers of the Inca Empire thousands of years ago.

The Atacama Desert in Chile is one of the driest places in the world. This **desert** is covered in sand and pebbles.

Caribbean
Sea

Caracas

LLANOS

Bogotá

Galapagos
Islands

Quito

Angel Falls

Marajó Island

Amazon

Manaus

A m a z o n

Machu Picchu

Lima

Andes Mountains

La Paz

Sucre

Atacama
Desert

Pacific
Ocean

Gran
Chaco

Santiago

Aconcagua

Buenos Aires

PAMPAS

Paraná

Patagonia

Falkland Islands

Cape Horn

Brazilian
Highlands

Brasília

São Paulo

Rio de Janeiro

Atlantic
Ocean

N
W   E
S

Map key
● city
★ mountain or other feature

South Georgia
Island

Angel Falls in Venezuela is the highest **waterfall** in the world.

•Rio de Janeiro is a large, beautiful **city** in Brazil. It is one of the most visited cities in South America.

South America has a lot of **farmland**. Farmers grow bananas, coffee beans, and cacao (*kuh KAY oh*), which is used to make chocolate.

Cape Horn is an area of land and islands at the southern tip of South America. A **cape** is a point of land that extends into the water.

•**Llamas** live in South America. People use llamas for their wool and to carry heavy loads through the mountains.

21

Pacific Islands

There are thousands of islands in the Pacific Ocean. Most of the islands are very far away from any continent. They do not make up a continent. Some islands are very big, but others are tiny piles of rock or sand that are only just above the water.

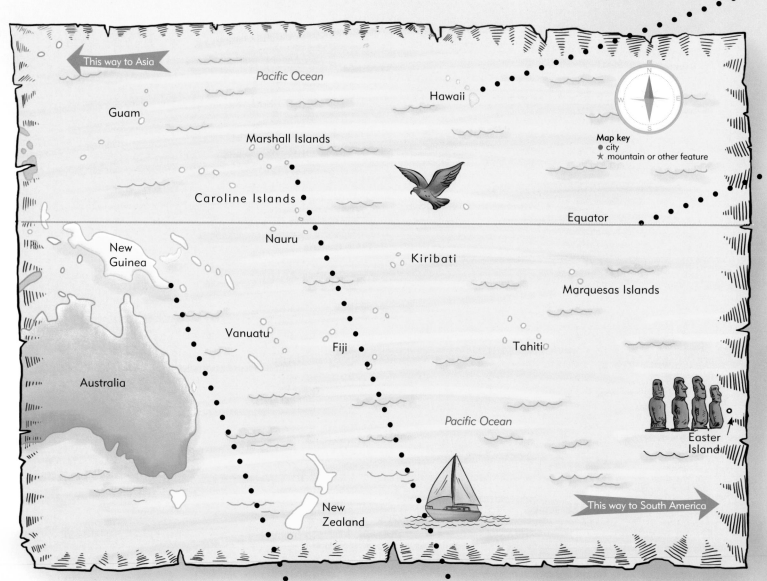

This way to Asia

Pacific Ocean

Hawaii

Guam

Map key
● city
★ mountain or other feature

Marshall Islands

Caroline Islands

Equator

Nauru

New Guinea

Kiribati

Marquesas Islands

Vanuatu

Fiji

Tahiti

Australia

Pacific Ocean

Easter Island

New Zealand

This way to South America

New Guinea is the largest **island** in the Pacific region and the second largest on Earth. Only Greenland is larger.

The Marshall Islands is a country made of dozens of **atolls** (AT olz). An atoll is a doughnut-shaped island made of coral reefs, which are made up of the skeletons of tiny sea animals called coral.

Hawaii is a state in the United States. There are volcanoes on the islands.

The imaginary line called the **equator** goes through the Pacific Islands region.

The land and weather are different across the Pacific Islands. Many of the islands have white-sand **beaches** and swaying palm trees.

Some islands have hot, thick jungles or snow-covered mountain peaks. Animals, like this Hawaiian honey-creeper bird, live on many of the islands.

Easter Island is famous for its large stone **statues**. People carved them hundreds of years ago. More than 600 of them are on the island.

It's a fact!

Only a few islands or island groups, such as Fiji, Hawaii, New Guinea, and New Zealand, have large numbers of people living on them.

In the classroom

Our Earth is a big place! We can learn more about the world and its continents at school.

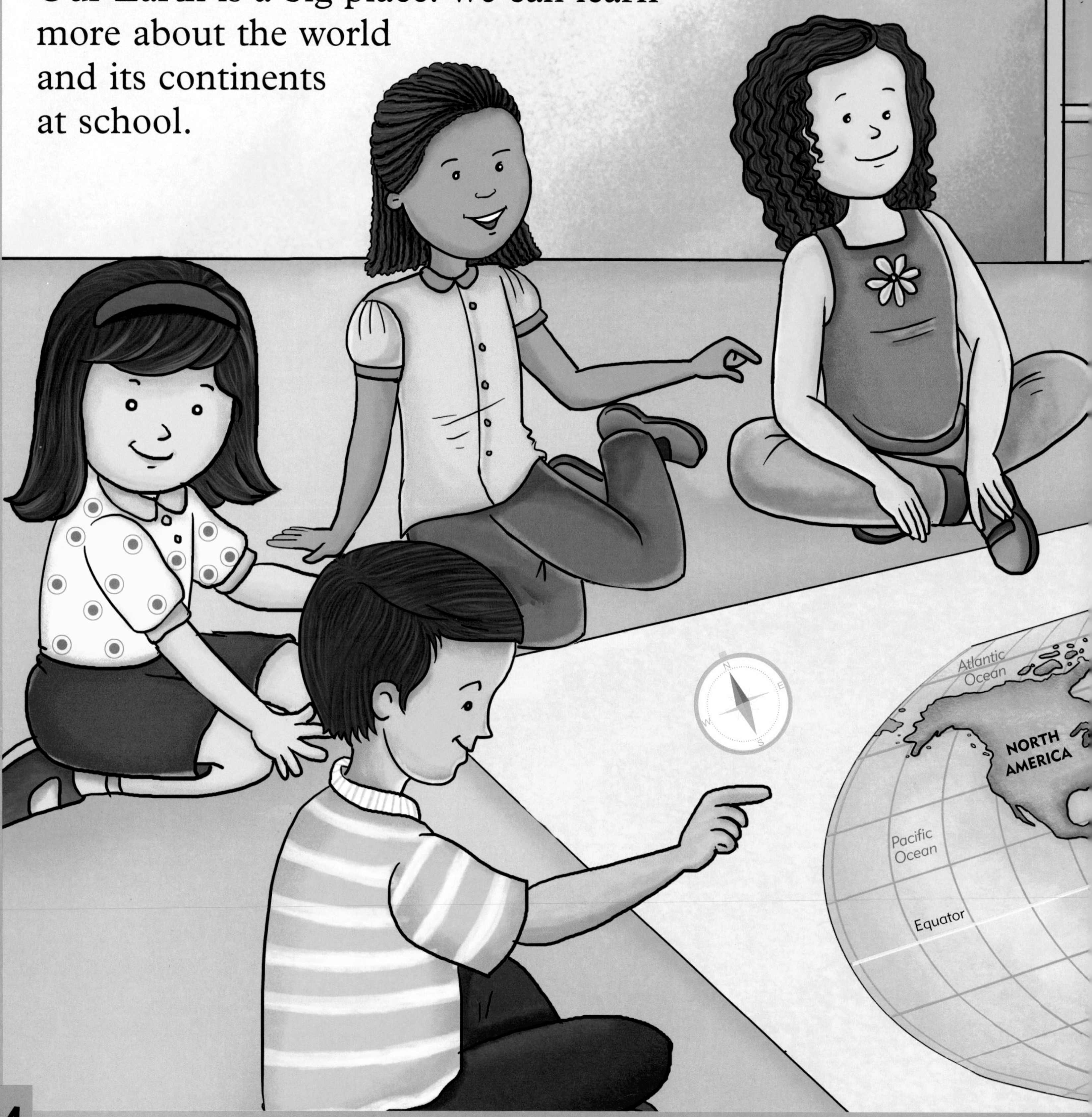

Atlantic Ocean
NORTH AMERICA
Pacific Ocean
Equator

Which two continents are all by themselves?

Words you know

Here are some words that you read earlier in this book. Say them out loud, then try to find the things in the picture.

continent   map
peninsula   ocean
compass   island

How many oceans are there?

25

Did you know?

The four seasons are reversed on opposite sides of the equator. When it is winter in the Northern Hemisphere, it is summer in the Southern Hemisphere.

Earth's plates move about 4 inches (10 centimeters) each year. That's about how fast human hair grows in a year!

Oceans cover about two-thirds of Earth's surface.

Farmlands cover more than a third of Earth's land. Growing crops is an important job for many people around the world.

Cartography (*kahr TOG ruh fee*) is the art and study of mapmaking. People who make maps are called cartographers.

Antarctica has almost all of Earth's ice.

Puzzles

Where's home?

Can you match each animal to the continent where it lives? Follow the lines to find out!

emperor penguin   **kangaroo**   **moose**

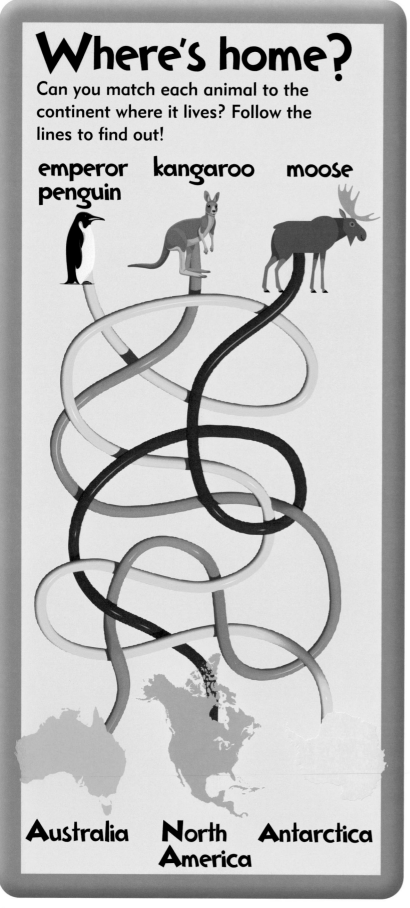

Australia   **North America**   **Antarctica**

Word jumble!

We've taken words from the book and mixed up the letters. Can you unscramble the letters to identify the word(s)?

1. saai

2. tonhr icamrae

3. staruaali

4. orepue

5. ciatanartc

6. uhsot cairema

7. fiarac

Answers on page 32.

Match up!

Match each word on the left with its picture on the right.

1. Pangaea

2. pyramid

3. llama

4. desert

5. volcano

6. mountain

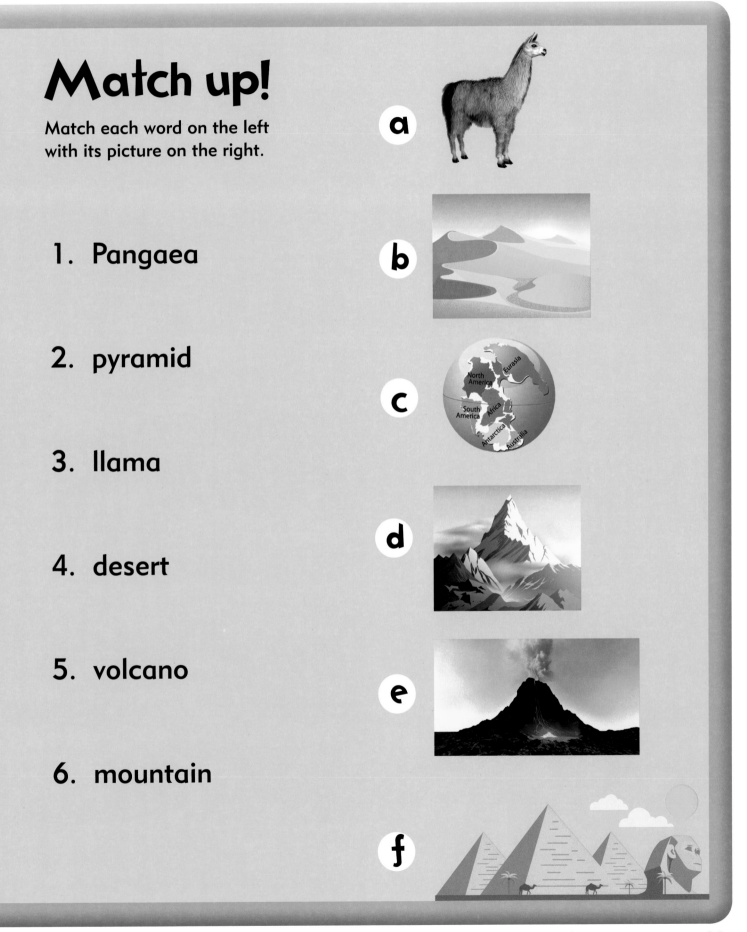

a

b

c

d

e

f

Answers on page 32.

True or false

Can you figure out which of these statements are true? Go to the page numbers given to help you find the answers.

1 Millions of years ago, most of Earth's land was probably joined in one large continent.
Go to page 7.

3 Thousands of islands are part of Europe.
Go to page 16.

4 Giza's pyramids were used to mark important days of the year.
Go to page 9.

2 The Sydney Opera House is in Asia.
Go to page 15.

5 Greenland is the world's largest island.
Go to page 19.

Answers on page 32.

Find out more

Books

Continents: What You Need to Know by Jill Sherman (Capstone Press, 2017)
From Africa, to Asia, to North America, take a tour of our world's continents. Find out all the need-to-know facts about climates, landforms, and unique features of each of these large land masses.

Continents in My World by Ella Cane (Capstone Press, 2013)
This beautifully illustrated volume examines our seven continents. It includes a list of books and websites for further research.

Earth's Continents by Irene Harris (Rosen Publishing Group, 2016)
This title encourages readers to explore Earth's continents and discover what makes each of them unique. Through age-appropriate text and engaging visuals, readers will learn about the continents' geography, landforms, climates, and wildlife.

This Is My Continent by Lisa Bullard (Lerner Publishing Group, 2016)
Noah and his babysitter, Ruby, are zooming around Earth in their spaceship. Ride along as they explore the people, places, and climates of the seven continents.

Websites

Dynamic Earth
http://www.learner.org/interactives/dynamicearth/index.html
This interactive lesson teaches students about the structure and movement of Earth. At the end of the lesson, students can take a quiz to test their knowledge.

Earth's Continental Plates
http://www.enchantedlearning.com/subjects/astronomy/planets/earth/Continents.shtmlZ
This *Enchanted Learning* site provides information about continental drift. It also contains quizzes and related links.

Geology for Kids
http://www.kidsgeo.com/geology-for-kids/0019-inside-of-earth.php
This site provides information about Earth's layers. It also contains information about the different types of rocks and landforms.

Ology
http://www.amnh.org/explore/ology/earth
This site sponsored by the American Museum of Natural History describes how Earth has changed over billions of years.

Answers

Puzzles
from pages 28 and 29

Word jumble!
1. Asia
2. North America
3. Australia
4. Europe
5. Antarctica
6. South America
7. Africa

Match up!
1. c
2. f
3. a
4. b
5. e
6. d

True or false
from page 30

1. true
2. false
3. true
4. false
5. true

Index